Prayers of Faith and Hope

Prayers for Christians to pray for Muslims during Ramadan

Leoma Gilley

Copyright © 2021 Leoma Gilley. ALL RIGHTS RESERVED. Reproduction of the whole or any part of the contents without written permission is prohibited. Any errors in the text are the responsibility of the author.

The cover photo taken by Leoma Gilley is the tomb of the Mahdi in Omdurman, Sudan. © 2021 by Leoma Gilley

Cover & book design: Howell Graphics
Editing: Jan Camburn

Unless otherwise indicated, all Scripture quotations are taken from the Holy Bible, New Living Translation, copyright 1996, 2004, 2007, 2015 by Tyndale House Foundation. Used by permission of Tyndale House Publishers, Inc., Carol Stream, Illinois 60188. All rights reserved.

Scripture quotations marked TPT are from The Passion Translation®. Copyright © 2017, 2018 by Passion & Fire Ministries, Inc. Used by permission. All rights reserved. thePassionTranslation.com.

Knoxville, Tennessee
www.crippledbeaglepublishing.com

Printed in the United States of America

Introduction

For about 20 years I lived in the Sudan. During that time, I became friends with many Muslims and came to respect them for trying to live out their faith. A number of them let me know that they were frustrated with Islam. However, there were limits to the questions they could ask before being considered heretics. Some desired to be devoted in their faith but over the years became disenchanted with their religion as, in their views, they didn't become better people. In the end, some decided to have no faith in God at all. These individuals may go through the motions of daily prayers and attendance at the mosque to pacify their family and friends, but there is no real effort to have a relationship with God. Of course, this is not representative of all Muslims, many of whom find deep meaning and comfort in their faith.

In Islam, there is always the uncertainty that one has "done enough" to get to heaven. Will their good deeds outweigh their bad deeds on the eternal scale? In Islam, there is no intermediary. There is no one to intercede for them before God the way Jesus intercedes for Christians. So today, many are searching for another answer, especially during the month of fasting known as Ramadan. Therefore, this is a wonderful time to offer our prayers to God on behalf of Muslims who are seeking the truth. As we pray during Ramadan, may God speak into the hearts of those who are searching and reveal himself to them as the Prince of Peace.

Acknowledgments

While I lived in a Muslim country for many years, there are still gaps in my understanding of the language and faith of Muslims. Therefore, I am deeply grateful for the corrections and suggestions to improve this work.

Dr. Peter Ford has taught Islamic Studies in multiple seminaries in East Africa. He is currently a professor at the Near East School of Theology in Beirut, Lebanon. Dr. Mike Kuhn has worked in a number of countries in the Middle East and is now Specialist in Missional Theology for the International Theological Educational Network (ITEN). In addition, I appreciate the input of Issa Isaac and Susie Isaac for their comments and suggestions. Each of these people have made suggestions to improve this work, and I'm grateful for their input. Any errors or misrepresentations remain the responsibility of the author.

Week 1

Blessing and Salvation

LORD, be merciful to the Muslim people and bless them in this season of Ramadan. May your face smile with favor on them as you make your ways known to them during this season. May your saving power be at work among Muslim people everywhere.

May the nations come to praise you, O God; yes, may all the Muslim people worship you in truth. Let the whole world sing for joy as Muslims come to know the one who governs the nations with justice and guides the people of the whole world into peace.

May the nations praise you, O God. Yes, may all the nations praise you.

Then the earth will yield its harvests, and God, our God, will richly bless all of us.

Yes, God, please bless us. May people all over the world come to respect, love, and revere you.

LORD, in your mercy, hear our prayer.

Based on Psalm 67

Clarity and Freedom

LORD, we come to you on behalf of Muslims
who have veils over their minds
so they can't understand
or sometimes even bear to hear
the truth of your love.
We realize that this "veil"
can be removed only by believing in Christ.
So, Lord, we ask that you open their minds
so that they may know the truth
and be set free from the burden
of following rules and regulations.
May they come into the freedom
of being children of God.
As they are freed to hear the truth,
may they see and reflect your glory, Lord,
becoming more like you as they are changed
into your glorious image.

LORD, in your mercy, hear our prayer.

Based on 2 Corinthians 3:14-18

Love for our Neighbor

ℒORD, help us to do to others,
particularly Muslims, whatever we would
like them to do to us.
Forgive us when we respond
with fear or apprehension, especially
when you teach through Scripture, repeatedly,
to "fear not." Help us to remember
the second command you gave:
"Love your neighbor as yourself."
May we strive to live in peace with everyone,
including Muslims. May we live out your love
in such a way that Muslims will see you in us.
Help us to live holy lives, for those who are holy are
marked as your people.

LORD, in your mercy, hear our prayer.

*Based on Matthew 7:12a, Matthew 22:39,
Hebrews 12:14*

Faith

LORD, we ask that Jesus will be the light
and the source of true salvation for Muslims.
Don't let them be afraid to learn about you
and trust in you, Jesus.
You will be a fortress,
protecting them from danger,
so help them to have the courage
to turn to you.
When others come to
attack and destroy them,
may the attackers stumble and fall.
Even if a mighty army surrounds those
who have turned to Jesus in faith,
don't let their hearts be afraid,
but rather keep them confident
in your power to save.

LORD, in your mercy, hear our prayer.

Based on Psalm 27:1-3

Protection

LORD, we ask that Muslims will realize
they are not yet part of your household
and community of faith because they
have not yet accepted Jesus' death
on the cross for their sins.
We ask that they desire to be part of your family,
to delight in your perfections
and to discover they are deeply loved.
We know they will likely face much opposition
if they do accept your invitation.
So, we ask that you conceal them
when troubles come and hide them
in your sanctuary. Place them on a high rock
out of reach of their persecutors.
Then they can hold their heads high
and offer praise to you with shouts of joy.

LORD, in your mercy, hear our prayer.

Based on Psalm 27:4-6

Loving All

LORD, you have told us
that you so loved the world, including Muslims,
that you gave your one and only Son
so that everyone who believes in Him
would not die but have eternal life.
We ask that you enable that good word
to reach all Muslims everywhere,
especially during this time of fasting
when they are seeking to know you.

LORD, in your mercy, hear our prayer.

Based on John 3:16

Personal Experience

FATHER, as Muslims seek you during this season,
may they find, like Job, that you can do anything
and no one can stop you.
Help them to recognize
all that you have done
by sending your only Son
to take the penalty for their sins.
May they discover you in a new way
and be able to say, "I had only heard
about you before,
but now I have seen you
with my own eyes and I repent."

LORD, in your mercy, hear our prayer.

Based on Job 42:2, 5-6

Week 2

Gracious Speech

FATHER, as we and other believers seek
to reach out to Muslims, help us to devote ourselves
to prayer with alert minds and thankful hearts.
Give us many opportunities to speak about your
mysterious plan concerning Christ.
We pray that we will proclaim
this message as
clearly as we should.

Help us to live wisely among those who
are not believers and to make the most of every
opportunity. May our conversations with Muslims
be gracious and attractive so that we will have
the right response for each one.

LORD, in your mercy, hear our prayer.

Based on Colossians 4:2-6

Seeking Truth

LORD, we pray that Muslims around the world
will learn to trust you with their whole hearts, not
depending on their own understanding
or the teachings they have received.
May they seek your will in all
they do and allow you to
show them the way to be right with you
and to receive eternal life.

LORD, in your mercy, hear our prayer.

Based on Proverbs 3:5-6

The Way

LORD, may Muslims come to know
that Jesus is the way, the truth, and the life,
and that no one can be acceptable to God
unless they come through him.
Please reveal to Muslims by your Holy Spirit
your Fatherly love that was
perfectly manifested
in Christ, your Son,
so that they too might
become sons and daughters.

LORD, in your mercy, hear our prayer.

Based on John 14: 6, 11

Need for a Savior

LORD, all of us, like sheep, have gone astray.
We have left your path to follow our own
ways. So, you laid all of our sins on
Jesus. May many Muslims
receive this sacrifice and find true forgiveness
and acceptance into your kingdom.

LORD, in your mercy, hear our prayer.

Based on Isaiah 53:6

Hunger and Thirst

LORD, we know that during these days of fasting
Muslims are hungry and thirsty.
May they hear your call to come and drink,
even if they have no money!
May they come and take
their choice of wine or milk; it's all free!
Why should they spend their money on food
that does not give strength?
Why pay for food that does them no good?
May they listen to you, God, and eat what is good.
They will enjoy the finest food.
May they come with their ears open.
May they listen, and find life.
May they seek you, Lord, while you can be found
and call on you while you are near.
Let them turn to you, Lord, so that you may have mercy
on them and they may find generous forgiveness.

LORD, in your mercy, hear our prayer.

Based on Isaiah 55:1-7

God's Holiness

LORD, reveal your holiness to Muslims—
the holy God that no human effort
or good work approaches.
May they understand that we are all
infected by sin and thus unclean.
When we display our righteous actions,
they are really nothing but filthy rags.
Like autumn leaves, we wither and fall and our sins
sweep us away with the wind.
But you have offered us salvation through Jesus,
who took our sins on himself and
paid the price for them.
May they receive this good message
and find hope and salvation.

LORD, in your mercy, hear our prayer.

Based on Isaiah 64:6

Thirst for God

As the deer longs for streams of water,
may Muslims long for you, O God.
May they thirst for you, the living God.
May they long to come and stand before you,
washed in the blood of the Lamb of God.
May they long to join in that
great procession to the house of God,
singing for joy and giving thanks
amid the sound of a great celebration.

LORD, in your mercy, hear our prayer.

Based on Psalm 42:1-4

Week 3

Peaceful Witnesses

GOD, bless those who work for peace.
Let them be known as the children of God.
Bless those who are persecuted for doing right, and
give them opportunities to speak peace into the
many situations of conflict and war
throughout the Muslim world.

Let us be salt and light to the Muslims around us.
May our good deeds shine out for all to see, so that
everyone will praise You, heavenly Father.

LORD, in your mercy, hear our prayer.

Based on Matthew 5:9-10, 16

Saved by Faith

*L*ORD, we acknowledge that we have ALL sinned.
We all fall short of your holy standard.
Yet, God, in your grace, you freely make us right
with you through Christ Jesus,
who has freed us from the penalty for our sins.
You gave Jesus to be the sacrifice for sin.
When we believe in him and what he did for us,
we are made right with you. Allow Muslims
to hear this message today.
May they find that following the religious practices
they have been taught can't fully satisfy
your standard of holiness.
But you have made a way for us

to meet that standard by faith
in our Savior, Jesus Christ.

LORD, in your mercy, hear our prayer.

Based on Romans 3:23-27

Way to Life

LORD, you have saved us and called us
to live a holy life, not because we deserve it
but because that was your plan
from before the beginning of time.
You have shown us your grace
through Christ Jesus and made all of this
plain to us by sending him to be our Savior.
Jesus is the one who broke the power of death
and showed us the way to life and immortality
through the Good News.
May Muslims discover this wonderful news
during this season as they search for you.

LORD, in your mercy, hear our prayer.

Based on 2 Timothy 1:9-10

True Fasting

*L*ORD, we confess that we all try to obey your commands, but we often fall short of the real meaning of the command and simply rely on the outward form to satisfy you. Remind all of us as to the true purpose of fasting.
This is the kind of fasting You want, O God:
"Free those who are wrongly imprisoned; lighten the burden of those who work for you.
Let the oppressed go free, and remove the chains that bind people.
Share your food with the hungry, and give shelter to the homeless.
Give clothes to those who need them, and do not hide from relatives who need your help.

Then salvation will come like the dawn, and your wounds will quickly heal. Your godliness will lead you forward, and the glory of the LORD will protect you from behind. Then when you call, I, the LORD, will answer.
'Yes, I am here.'"

LORD, in your mercy, hear our prayer.

Based on Isaiah 58:6-9

Persecution

LORD, we pray for your mercy on
those believers who, though once Muslims,
have trusted in you and are now being persecuted
as they are ostracized from families, excluded
from educational and vocational opportunities,
and may face physical and verbal abuse.
We pray that they will not be afraid
of those who want to harm them,
for we know that no one can touch the soul.
May they fear only you, O God,
because you alone have power
over both soul and body.
May these believers remember your promise
that the very hairs of their heads are numbered.
They are valuable in your sight
and do not need to be afraid,
whatever happens.

LORD, in your mercy, hear our prayer.

Based on Matthew 10:28-31

Coming to Faith

LORD, for all those Muslims
who will become your children,
we ask that you watch over and care for them
and bring them to yourself.
Build them up even when others
try to tear them down.
Plant them firmly in your Word
even as others try to uproot them.
Give them hearts to understand
their need for forgiveness
and to receive the sacrifice
you made for them, Lord.
May they be your people, and
may you be their God.
May they wholeheartedly follow you.

LORD, in your mercy, hear our prayer.

Based on Jeremiah 24:6-7

Understanding

LORD, may all Muslims
who search for you
find you and be filled
with joy and gladness in you.
May those who shout, "God is great!"
come to know and love
your salvation so that
they truly understand
how great you are.

LORD, in your mercy, hear our prayer.

Based on Psalm 70:4

Week 4

Seek and Find

LORD, you have promised that those who look for you wholeheartedly will find you and that you will end their captivity and restore them. Lord, for those Muslims today who are searching for you, we ask that when they pray you will listen. You know the plans you have for these searchers, plans for good and not for disaster, to give them a future and a hope.

LORD, in your mercy, hear our prayer.

Based on Jeremiah 29:11-14

Hope of Heaven

LORD, we ask that you reveal yourself to many
Muslims during this season. As you do that,
may they know that their Redeemer lives,
and he will return to earth at the end of time
as Lord and Savior and Judge. After their
bodies decay, when in their new bodies,
they will see you, God! They will
see you for themselves with their
own eyes. May they be overwhelmed
by this prospect and
truly worship you.

LORD, in your mercy, hear our prayer.

Based on Job 19:25-27

Awareness of Sin

LORD, we acknowledge that we are all weak in our human nature. As we pray for Muslims during this time, we ask that they realize how they have become slaves to impurity and lawlessness. As they feel ashamed of their failure to live up to your high standard and realize they are slaves to the power of sin, bring them out of this situation. May they hear your warning and your promise that "the wages of sin is death, but the free gift of God is eternal life through Christ Jesus our Lord."

LORD, in your mercy, hear our prayer.

Based on Romans 6:19-23

Helplessness

LORD, we pray for those Muslims who want to do what is right but can't do it. Instead, they do and tolerate what they hate. Help them see that it is sin living in them that causes them to do these unwanted actions. May they understand that nothing good lives in them, in their sinful nature. They want to do what is right but can't. They want to do what is good but don't. They don't want to do wrong but do it anyway, and they can't save themselves.

Thank you, LORD, for freeing all believers from the power of sin that leads to death. Because of Jesus' death on the cross, we are no longer under condemnation but can live in the power of the life-giving Spirit.

LORD, in your mercy, hear our prayer.

Based on Romans 7:15-24; 8:1-2

Community

$\mathcal{L}$ORD, as children of God, you do not
want us to serve with a spirit of religious duty,
leading into the fear of never being good enough.
Instead, you have given us the spirit
of full acceptance, enfolding us into your family.
So, during this time of fasting, may Muslims
realize that you are inviting them into the freedom
of becoming your beloved sons and daughters.

LORD, in your mercy, hear our prayer.

Romans 8:15-16 (TPT)

Night of Power - Laylat al Qadr

Visions and Dreams

LORD, on this night, Muslims seek guidance from
you. They celebrate the revelation of the Qur'an,
which has tied them to many rules and regulations.
We know that the law simply
shows us how sinful we are.
Thank you for showing us the way to be made
right with you is not about keeping laws.
Thank you that we can be made right with you
by placing our faith in Jesus Christ.
Thank you that this fact is true
regardless of who we are.
May many Muslims seek you tonight.
May they be blessed with seeing you in person
(the ultimate revelation of God)
and find your salvation.

LORD, in your mercy, hear our prayer.

Romans 3:20-23

Hope

LORD, we ask that you will free Muslims
from the chains of sin and death
and bring them into the freedom
of a life led by the Holy Spirit.
May your Spirit control their minds
and bring them life and peace.
As they invite you into their lives,
take control and adopt them
into your amazing family.
Then they will know the joy
of being your children,
heirs of your glory.

LORD, in your mercy, hear our prayer.

Based on Romans 8:9-17

Response to Suffering

LORD, we know that if Muslims decide
to follow you and to accept Jesus' sacrifice for them,
there will likely be persecution.
So, we ask that you give them the confidence and
assurance that if you, God, are for them,
who can ever be against them?
Since you didn't spare your Son
but gave him up for us all, you, God,
will give them everything they need.
They will have right standing with you,
so they will not be accused or condemned.
Jesus, who died and was raised from the dead,
will be pleading for them and for us
as he sits in the place of honor in the heavens.
May Muslim converts know
that overwhelming victory is theirs
through Christ who loves them.

LORD, in your mercy, hear our prayer.

Based on Romans 8:31-37

Feast of Breaking the Fast, Eid al-Fitr

The Lamb of God

As Muslims are eating during this feast,
may they learn how Jesus took some bread,
blessed it, broke it into pieces,
and gave it to his disciples, saying,
"Take this and eat it, for this is my body."
And he took a cup of wine and gave thanks,
gave it to them and said, "Each of you drink from it,
for this is my blood, which confirms the covenant
between God and his people. It is poured out as a
sacrifice to forgive the sins of many."
May this ultimate sacrifice and covenant
be real in the lives of Muslims
and draw them to you.

LORD, in your mercy, hear our prayer.

Based on Matthew 26:26-28

Author Biography

Leoma lived and worked in the Sudan for about 20 years. During that time, she lived among, worked with, and developed deep friendships with many Muslims. As a Christian, she would like to see her friends and colleagues come to faith in Jesus Christ. This book of prayers, takenfrom Scripture, is offered as a way for others to join in to pray for the Muslim world during the special month of fasting called Ramadan.

Other Works by Leoma Gilley

The Still Small Voice of Love: A journey into a deeper relationship with Jesus

In this thought and prayer-provoking devotional, author Leoma Gilley leads readers by example as she explores Scripture and listens for God's responses. Readers are not only welcomed into Leoma's heart, but they also see the heart of Jesus in His intimate responses to her fears, needs, questions, and longings. After each devotional, readers are prompted to follow the Lectio Divina method of Scriptural study to expand and deepen their own personal relationships with Jesus Christ.

Praying for Big Things

Leoma Gilley has a deep reverence for the Bible and a desire to pray in more effective ways. Having been challenged by a colleague to pray for situations in the world that are really serious, she sought to develop prayers based on scripture to pray God's words back to him. This book doesn't cover everything, but it is a beginning, and Leoma hopes it will help to enrich and deepen your prayer life as it has hers.

Prayers of Confessions for Lent

During an Ash Wednesday service, many areas for confession were mentioned. It seemed more reflection was needed. These prayers are the result of those reflections.

www.ingramcontent.com/pod-product-compliance
Lightning Source LLC
Chambersburg PA
CBHW071424070526
44578CB00003B/681